AN IDEA APPEARED

First Published in Great Britain 2015 by Mirador Publishing

First edition: 2015

A copy of this work is available through the British Library.

ISBN: 978-1-910530-64-1

Mirador Publishing
Mirador
Wearne Lane
Langport
Somerset
TA10 9HB

An Idea Appeared

By

Michael Haley

Introduction

So I'd finished writing my novels, "Chelmsford 2012 - Many Hearts One Mind" and "First City of Essex - Many Diversions One Destination" They'd been published and had sold millions (Ho! Ho!).

Then my mind turned to something else. I'd been writing poems and songs since I was a spotty teenager, and stories perhaps since I was a wrinkly pensioner. I therefore decided to attempt to compile and edit all of my writings of any quality from the very beginning. Like many of my writing projects this seemed to grow exponentially until it occurred to me that the editing and compiling into an acceptable format was going to take many months of hard work. So I decided that in the interim I would put together a little collection of poems and songs illustrating the full range of my creations. That would then give me a lot more time to continue to work on the big job called "Tall Words on a Wall".

Perhaps this little collection could be regarded as an aperitif, or an hors d'oeuvres, or even an amuse bouche, but then again it's none of them because there aren't any French songs or poems included. Whatever the classification, I hope you enjoy this little sampler, and come back for more.

About the Author

Michael Haley was born and raised in Essex and considers himself to be a true Essex man. He has lived in the Chelmsford for 35 years. His working life was spent in computers and telecommunications.

He bought his first "proper" guitar, a 12-string acoustic, in 1968. He taught himself to play, and intends to carry on doing so until he gets it right. He has been writing poems, songs and short stories since he was 18.

Michael is a divorcee who lives alone, and has a daughter Michelle, and two grandsons Callum and Connor. An ardent fan of Chelmsford City Football Club, he is a regular attendee at many local writing groups. His favourite poets are the songwriters Bob Dylan and Roy Harper.

Most of his creative emphasis has so far been in writing songs, but he recently had 2 novels published by Mirador and they are available through Amazon.

"Chelmsford 2012 - Many Hearts One Mind"

Is the first novel in a two-part series and covers the period from February to June that year.

ISBN 978-1-910104-76-7

"First City of Essex - Many Diversions One Destination"

Is the second novel covering the period from July to December 2012.

ISBN 978-1-910530-04-7

The novels tell a fictional tale with a backdrop of real places in Chelmsford, in Essex and in Britain in the great and unforgettable year 2012. The unpredictable weather patterns, the granting of City status to Chelmsford, the Queen's Diamond Jubilee events, the London Olympics, and a range of issues local to Chelmsford all play a part. The actions and interactions of the characters are a soap opera about people, good or bad, cheerful or sad, going about their lives the best way they can, and making their way through. This is a tale about real hopes and dreams, social and personal issues in the 21st century, and things that we all care about.

Future projects include:

"Tall Words on Wall"

A compilation of poems, songs and stories assembled in a biographical framework.

Expected to be available for publication Autumn 2015.

"Angel's Rainbow"

A novel about Michael Hartson, a financial whiz kid working in the City of London, who finds himself on a journey to becoming an angel. His transformation begins when he misses an important meeting and subsequently encounters a tramp in the local park. As an apprentice he must undertake a number of very difficult tasks in the Earthly realm in order to qualify as a fully fledged angel and earn his wings.

Expected to be available for publication Spring 2016.

Dedication

I am indebted to a number of people for encouragement, help and inspiration.

Many thanks first of all to the members of the White Horse Writer's Group, especially the incomparable Estella Boxell-Hutson, but also Kerry Barr, Margaret King, Henry Cotton, Gill Adams, Christine McDonald and Sheena Cundy.

Many thanks also to the members of the Maldon Writer's Group - Pat Harris, Anna Webb, Robert Chatterton, Christopher Smith, and Alison Dixon.

Thanks to Maggie Freeman whose little poetry book ,"Singing for Mr Bear" inspired me to compile something similar in "An Idea Appeared".

Finally I am most grateful to Alan Webb for his invaluable proof reading, and getting me to look at my poetry in a completely different way.

Words and Ideas

"When pen came to paper...."

1. An idea appeared,	Written13th September 1999
2. Stirring words,	First written circa 1980 and completed August 2002
3. Word games,	Written14th September 1999

I thought this would be a good starter for the selection of poems in my little book because these 3 items are all really about the same things. Sometimes, as a writer, you might want to put some meaningful words together while suffering from a loss of inspiration. It's a bit of clever trickery really, to recover from the inspiration block (but not lack of creativity) that's leaving you in the doldrums, by reverting to writing about things involved in the process of writing itself.

An idea appeared

When pen came to paper an idea appeared;
At first just a verse, or a phrase that endeared;
Some words in a row that sounded quite clever,
complementing each other by standing together.
Some lines once refined and a rhyme neatly timed;
a discreet little metre, a sing-song-like chime,
Then an idea that swelled, blossomed, evolved,
until all the loose ends were tried, tied, and solved,
and every fine detail was tested and cleared;
When pen came to paper an idea appeared.

Stirring words

As memories cascade from me, nostalgia cries to be set free;
Forgotten dreams and fantasies return from my infinity.
The clock has ticked; long ages spent; so seldom inspiration sent.
To steal the poet's zeal again; let magic gems flow from the pen;
to tear the dusty sheets apart with stirring words, stirring words,
stirring words, straight from the heart -
With stirring words, stirring words, stirring words, straight from the heart.

So sad the passing bloom of youth that held reality aloof,
For as we grow long in the tooth sad eyes reveal distorted truth.
Experience, the saving grace, to take enthusiasm's place.
It is by choice and not by chance, from circumstances thoughts advance,
And so by chance and not by choice, words may arrive, may arrive,
Words may arrive to raise a voice -
Words may arrive, may arrive, words may arrive to raise a voice.

If only I was young again, with yearning heart burning as then;
To set new milestones in my mind, adventures of a different kind.
Just lurking in the atmosphere - a spark to light a new idea.
By accident, not by design, sweet reminiscence fills my time,
But by design, not accident, my time is lost, time is lost,
My time is lost as time is spent,
My time is lost, time is lost, my time is lost as time is spent.

Word games

The power of the written word
Can frighten, enlighten, or disturb;
Can emphasise, comfort, disarm or inspire,
Provide the spark to light a fire.

Words are a weapon,
Words are a shield,
Words are a haven,
Words are a wheel.

Words can impassion,
Words can inflame,
Words can incite,
Or apportion blame.

Words can be ugly,
Words can be crude,
Words can be coarse,
Words can be rude.

Words can be pretty,
Words can be smart,
Words can bring tears
Or touch at your heart.

And when those words are softly spoken,
With open heart and silence broken,
They stir the sweetest dark emotion
Or reveal the depth of true devotion.

Words are a comfort,
Words can soothe,
Words can be false
Or tell the truth.

Words can punish,
Words can be cruel,
Words can admonish
For breaking the rules.

Words can be elegant,
Words can be strong,
Sometimes irrelevant
And sometimes just wrong.

Words can be short,
Words can be long,
Words are music,
Words are a song.

Perhaps words can set free our fears,
Release a flood of guarded tears
Or call to mind forgotten friends;
Smooth a path, or make amends.

Words are an arrow,
Words can appease,
Words are a puzzle;
A riddle, a tease.

Words can say love,
Words can say hate,
Words can say go,
Words can say wait.

Words can be funny,
Words can be mad,
Words can be tragic,
Words can be sad.

Words can be wasted
Or a well-chosen few,
And sometimes it's true
That no words will do.

Words can mend or break your heart,
Pull us together or push us apart;
Words can move mountains,
Words can dam streams;
Shatter illusions or build up our dreams.

But the power of the written word
Is not surprising or absurd,
Within this power we stand assured -
The pen is mightier than the sword.

Time and the Seasons

"The clock of the seasons goes round and around."

1. Clock of the Seasons	written 2nd January 2003
2. Tick Tock	written 2nd April 1999
3. Shadows	written circa 1996
4. Winter Song	written 27th October 2000
5. Oh to be an Englishman	written 8th March 2013
6. Life in a stolen moment	written 27th March 1999

The unstoppable passage of time and the consequential turning over of the seasons are obviously linked and are an inspirational well that can never run dry. Happy, sad, wistful and morbid; the two subjects of time and the seasons can prove to be an inspiration for all these moods - and many more.

Clock of the Seasons

Round and around, round and around,
The clock of the seasons goes round and around;
So praise be to he who holds the gold key
in the stock of the lock for the spring to be wound.
So praise be to he, forever to see
the clock of the seasons goes round and around.

In a cold, pale, low sky, a gold watery sun
Slow rises to say a new day's just begun;
Cruel deep winds blow and high-heaped snows fall,
So the white Christmas winter is the hope for us all
And eerie, thin shadows scratch their names on the ground
As the clock of the seasons goes round and around.

Round and around, round and around,
The clock of the seasons goes round and around;
So praise be to he who holds the gold key
in the stock of the lock for the spring to be wound.
So praise be to he, forever to see
the clock of the seasons goes round and around.

Wild cherry blossoms as morning birds sing
A warm, welcome song to our fair maiden of Spring.
She spins and she weaves sweet new grass and green leaves
As a carpet of bluebells sweeps under the trees;
And all God's small creatures awake safe and sound
As the clock of the seasons goes round and around.

Round and around, round and around,
The clock of the seasons goes round and around;
So praise be to he who holds the gold key
in the stock of the lock for the spring to be wound.
So praise be to he, forever to see
the clock of the seasons goes round and around.

When a fire-flame red sky 'ere fall of warm night
Paints Heaven's blue yonder for our shepherd's delight,
And butterflies flutter and bumble bees hover
In the shade of a willow by a lazy green river,
Then Summertime rides her long merry-go-round,
As the clock of the seasons goes round and around.

Round and around, round and around,
The clock of the seasons goes round and around;
So praise be to he who holds the gold key
in the stock of the lock for the spring to be wound.
So praise be to he, forever to see
the clock of the seasons goes round and around.

Now mellow fruits ripen down blackberry lanes,
Summer bids us farewell for strong winds and sharp rains,
Wild harvest moon horses under shooting stars dance
And fairies cast circles in the damp, dewy grass,
And reds, golds, and yellows now shower the ground
As the clock of the seasons goes round and around.

Round and around, round and around,
The clock of the seasons goes round and around;
So praise be to he who holds the gold key
in the stock of the lock for the spring to be wound.
So praise be to he, forever to see
the clock of the seasons goes round and around.

Tick Tock

Tick went the slow, slow slip of the sound,
Till the tock at the end of the tick came around,
And the slot in between, when the spring unwound,
Clocked an endless slice of a life unbound.

With a tick and a tock, and a fairground bound,
Rock and roll, up and down, on the merry-go-round,
And pick at the lock, as the hands spin round,
Now the rhythm it clicks to a quickening sound.

Tick-tock, tick-tock, tick-tock, resound
As the hands on the clock non-stop turnaround,
With gathering speed and clattering sound,
Tick-tock, tick-tock, tick-tock, spellbound.

Ticka-tocka, ticka-tocka, ticka-tocka, tock,
And tock follows tick as tick follows tock,
To the ever mocking, ever knocking ticking of the clock,
Going on tick-tocking and tock-ticking to a stop.

Shadows

Tall fleeting narrow shadows softly fall
And silent slowly slip across green Summer evening hills.
Hills, so timelessly serene;
Unchained by greed of human needs,
Untamed by careless crude machines,
Inflamed by virgin purity.

Winter Song

The naked tree, a frosty carcass
Stripped of all its leaves,
Perched among the barrenness;
The blanket Winter weaves,
Trapped under frozen glassy skies,
Choked with new-spun snows,
Aching in the watery sunshine
Of the Winter's throes.

Desolation shrouds the hillsides,
Bared and ravaged shell.
How long, how long 'til Spring's sweet chorus
Breaks the Arctic spell?
Deep, so deep the landscape sleeps
Upon the diamond Earth,
Through the echoes of the Summer,
'Til the Spring's rebirth.

When Mother Earth awakes again,
From feelings Winter gripped;
The ancient cycle turns to find
Her icy hand has slipped,
Now just a blurred reflection in
The season's passing page,
When Springtime celebrates again
Escape from Winter's rage.

Oh to be an Englishman

(With thanks to Robert Browning for the inspiration of his first line)

Oh to be an Englishman, now that Summer's here,
Sitting in the Red Lion garden, sipping lukewarm beer,
A beer with depth and flavour, that packs a real ale punch,
English cheeses to savour, in my English Ploughman's lunch;
A warm breeze oozing through the trees,
The touch of sunshine on my face,
A hum of buzzing bumble bees,
Summer flowers in full blaze,
The Morris Men in merry dance,
Tradition from afar still near,
Oh to be an Englishman, now that Summer's here.

Life in a stolen moment

In the moment you were born
There was no time,
For you,
There was no past,
And without the power
to fathom further
the future was not real.
There was only you,
There was only now,
There was only you, there was only now.
You who simply cried "I want!"
"I want to be loved."
"I want to be safe and warm."
The now that screamed, "Here I am!"
Scared, hungry or in pain,
There was only you,
There was only now,
There was only you, there was only now.

Thus far
There were no days,
There had been no nights,
Just being, seeing, feeling.
You cannot remember
because,
There was no time.
There was only you,
There was only now,
There was only you, there was only now.

The first glimpse of time
came with light and dark,
Daytime, night-time, teatime,
Bath-time, bedtime;
Time to eat or go to sleep,
Time to play.
You were small,
Your sense of time was smaller still.

One day when you were two they sang,
"Happy Birthday to You",
Up 'til then all you knew,
Of numbers, was one;
Then other numbers came -
Three, four and five,
And they said it is time
to go to learn more.

Things were changing;
There had been some weeks,
There had been some months,
There had been few years,
But mostly days and nights;
Then they divided up your daytimes;
Into lessons and playtimes,
Weekends and school-times;
And at the end of each day -
Night times.

The important time was coming closer,
Coming all too soon;
Soon you would surrender your freedom,
Willingly surrender
To be a prisoner of numbers,
A captive of time;
To be a slave, slave to the clock,
An incessant tick-tock,
A servant of now, then or when.

Still more numbers came,
Bigger numbers games
To measure and to count
In increasing amounts.
Times tables were learned,
Your bridges were burned;
And then you discovered
Those smaller bits beckoned;
To break up your days into hours,
Your hours into minutes and seconds.

And the hands on the clock,
Made seconds tick-tock;
Passed moments by,
Making time fly.
And they taught you well,
To tell the time,
But to tell the time what?
To stay?
To go away?
To leave your day?
Soon, on your wrist,
You carried time as a burden.

And watchmakers knew,
A watch does not watch you,
You watch it!
To measure your moments
as they fall together,
Like grains of sand,
To build your lifetime,
On some shaky foundation;
One day to be swept away
by a relentless tidal wave.

Then, for some time you have a past
and you foresee a future;
But the Now
always vanishes in an instant.
You can live in the moment,
But you cannot capture it;
It is here and then it's gone,
You measure time
and have to pay homage to it.

But one day, no one can say when,
Your time will come -
Come to an end;
There will be no more time.
The past will have passed
while you hesitated.
The future will be gone;
All at once dissipated,
And for an instant, once again
There will be only you,
There will be only now,
Only you, and only now.

And then after,
Forever after,
Forever and never,
For evermore
There will be only then.

But you will be free,
Released from captivity,
No longer a hostage;
Set free
into nothing,
To be no one,
For no time;
For time without end

Loss and Lament

"In worship to the restless spirits of creation and always."

1. November	Written 14th November 1998
2. Lost Child	Written 8th January 2006
3. May Day! May Day!	Written May 1996
4. Everlasting Light	Written 1st October 2000

I've scrambled this little 4- parter together, but perhaps each of them could be dispersed fairly easily into the other selections. However, as I've got a specific heading of "Love" later, it occurred to me that maybe a section for "Loss and Lament" provided a healthy balance. In these 4 lamenting poems/songs I mourn the passing of a season, agitate over the nightmare of a solitary child left alone on a beach, illustrate a real life experience where someone I did not know passed away, and then look for spirituality in the end of a love affair.

November

November, harsh frost, freezing ground,
November, tumbling leaves turning brown.
The Summer now lies fallen,
A cold chill cuts the air,
New season's loom spins out thin snares
to capture and leave bare.

November, tall flames became a cinder glow,
November, awaits first falls of Winter's snow.
Like echoes in the spells of fate;
Sweet passion staggers in and dies,
November's whims, sly they lie in wait,
To strike their savage, sharp surprise.

November, short days, growing cold,
November, Autumn's secrets to unfold.
With restless soul and sleepless mind;
A candle's flicker flame remains,
The hope for all who fall in love,
Alone, endure a lover's pain.

Lost Child

In the pale yellow light of a long seaside evening,
On a nearly empty beach as a fading sunset dies,
Among the salty tasting tang of dampening sea breezes
There calls an eerie, lonely sound that pulls my urgent gaze.

Under the lazy swoop and swirl of searching seagull glides,
Merging all too easily with the softly lapping waves,
Along a sandy twilight waterline is where I faintly spy
A lost child, solitary, crying by the sea.

Tears are smothered in the swell,
Cries are muted by the sounds,
She stands there and looks around;
There's no one to be seen.

And as the ever moving hand of dark, relentless night
Sweeps away the last few rays of Summer's dying light,
A frantic mess of deepening shadows swallows up the sound
And carries her away to be in the warmth of welcome arms.

Bright day is soon abandoned to cool night's persuading charms,
Her failing soft hold now releases, crying ceases, she is safe;
And all that remains in stillness are gently lapping waves,
In worship to the restless spirits of creation and always.

May Day! May Day!

I watched and I listened for six hours long,
But at the end of the battle, when her last breath was gone,
They'd fought to save someone that they never met,
Trapped in the blackness of a tightening net,
Trapped in the blackness of a tightening net.

Just a few nights before they'd done the same for me,
Confounded the Reaper, changed my destiny,
These unsung angels and heroines all,
Who fight the Grim Reaper whenever he calls,
Who fight the Grim Reaper wherever he calls.

Sure I always knew life was precious it's true,
But I hadn't a clue how hard they fought for you,
And if they then lost as the battle ensued,
How they cried for that someone that they never knew,
How they cried for that someone that they never knew.

Everlasting Light

Found a fairy circle in the meadow,
Fresh and wet, with new morning dew,
So I stepped inside this magic little spotlight,
Made a wish, and then I thought of you.
Then turned around one, and two, and three,
Warmed in watery Summer's-gone sunshine,
Sealed the wish into my achin' heart,
And now it's just a matter of time.

Beside a secret garden's wishing well,
Almost hidden by a tangled leafy hue;
We kissed, and then I tossed a lucky penny,
Made a wish, and then I thought of you.
We held our breath while waiting for the splash
of my penny falling far below,
Until the rippling echoes of the water
told me now it's time for you to go.

You left a howling hollow in my heart;
An empty vacant space, so icy blue,
I wandered lonely underneath the tall skies,
Whispered a prayer, and then I thought of you.
Then shivered in the green, tree shade;
My broken heart was pounding fit to burst;
I saw a chequered road stretching out afar
and disappearing into distant dust.

Now a holy beacon shines my way;
A bright guiding light there to see me through;
And as sure as sunset follows sunrise everyday
I say a prayer, and then I think of you.
Amongst the busy turmoil of my days,
Against the darkest forces in my nights,
Leaving pale and faded shadows to the past;
Towards the everlasting light.

War and Conflict

"It's only one small step, just another grain of sand."

1. Armistice — Written November 1998

2. Kosovo — Written June 1999

3. Clear September Sky - Part 2 - Answer — Written 29th October 2002 & 4th December, 2002

4. Clear September Sky - Part 1 - Question — Written 4th December 2002 & 7th August, 2003

5. Elegy — Written circa 1980 & amended in 1997, added to, March 2001 and finished 31st December 2001

6. Ghost of a Ploughman (Fair Poppy Fields of France) — Written 12th September 2012

Is peace for the world an elusive and unattainable illusion? War and conflict are almost accepted constants of human civilisation. Here's a selection including two poems about World War One, two poems covering the tricky subject of 9/11, one about a hideous, fairly recent conflict resulting in ethnic cleansing, and in "Elegy" a more cryptic and obscure piece of writing about the processes of conflict and in particular the real prospects of ending all life on Earth in a nuclear holocaust.

Armistice

My boy's years behind me, once eager and bold,
For King and for country, for freedom I'm told,
Kitchener wants me, with courage inspired;
to beat down the Kaiser, and save the Empire.

We marched off to war, patriotic and proud,
Girls cheered and threw flowers, bands played long and loud,
But excitement soon done, the ugly truth dawned;
For battle in Flanders, unlearned and un-warned.

In waterlogged trenches, all barbed wire and mud,
Machines guns and mustard gas, wasted our blood,
Deafened and deadened and shell-shocked and spent,
As four year's of comrades in arms came and went.

In safety remote great generals planned,
Sacrifices relentless for acres of land,
At Ypres and Verdun and along the Somme,
In savage abandon, shells, bullets and bombs.

Then orders came down, "Attack! Boys, Attack!"
As dark stench of death hung heavy and black,
And choking back tears, with no chance for goodbyes,
I watched helpless as brave men were blown to the skies.

All the king's horses and all the king's men,
Couldn't patch Charlie together again,
In my pocket his diary to give to his wife,
Not much to show for such a young life.

Today there's a strange eerie sense in the air,
There's rumours an armistice has been declared,
Have the Germans surrendered? Have we won victory?
Is it over for good, or just temporary?

So they've worked out a truce, timed precise to the minute;
A ceasefire dreamed up by a war-monger cynic.
In some mad numbers game eleven was chosen,
Fate marched to that standstill, the instant was frozen.

Though sadder and wiser we came home as men,
A land fit for heroes they promised us then.
A fast fading band who fought a lost cause
now remembers the war an end to all wars.

Kosovo

Homes blaze in the village, abandoned, destroyed,
Meagre possessions bundled crudely for flight,
Away scurried in haste to hide in the forests,
Past shallow quick graves of victims new murdered.

Tear-stained frightened children, with smoke-blackened faces
stare blankly eyes pleading in hunger and fear;
At once still relieved to be spared from the slaughter,
But fearful the future uncertain does stand.

No longer the peace of plain rustic existence,
The clock of the seasons, the harvest and plough,
Pale refugee faces tell tortured dark stories
as vanquished and beaten, they make for safe haven.

To the victors the treasure, fine wines in good measure,
Where death and destruction have won hollow gains,
To drive the sad peasants from the lands of their birth,
Their too willing war, genocide, and scorched earth.

With brutal abandon and killing at random,
So cruel and depraved the ground forces waged.
As tools of black terror raged death in green valleys,
Blowing wild through the land like the wrath of false gods.

Clear September Sky - part 2 - the Answer

Just another Trader's day
In a clear September sky,
Where the tallest stone and steel trees proudly grow.
Deadly arrow's suicide aim,
For some heathen godless name,
Sends trees crashing to the streets far below.

It's only one small step, just another grain of sand
From Once upon a Time, to Never-Never Land.
All the castles in the air, all the fallout from the blast,
All the secrets that we keep, all the stones that we may cast,
Still mean nothing in the end, have no reason and no rhyme,
Falling out of Never-Never Land to Once upon a Time,
Falling out of Never-Never Land to Once upon a Time.

The sand angel's evil hand,
Hurled a curse upon this land,
Swirling shadows dark to hide the devil's breath.
At ground zero's great impasse,
Wise eyes through the looking glass
Spied the angel's new name, became "Death".

It's only one small step, just another grain of sand
From Once upon a Time, to Never-Never Land.
All the castles in the air, all the fallout from the blast,
All the secrets that we keep, all the stones that we may cast,
Still mean nothing in the end, have no reason and no rhyme,
Falling out of Never-Never Land to Once upon a Time,
Falling out of Never-Never Land to Once upon a Time.

And as long as Freedom lives;
Must we forget? Must we forgive?
Stone-hearted men who bend the lens of time,
For they stand on shifting sands;
May forever they be damned,
For our Lord assured, "Vengeance is mine!"

It's only one small step, just another grain of sand
From Once upon a Time, to Never-Never Land.
All the castles in the air, all the fallout from the blast,
All the secrets that we keep, all the stones that we may cast,
Still mean nothing in the end, have no reason and no rhyme,
Falling out of Never-Never Land to Once upon a Time,
Falling out of Never-Never Land to Once upon a Time.

Clear September Sky - part 1 - Question

Action and reaction in line forever stand,
Jump from the bridge oblivion,
Into a blood-stained hand,
Whilst empathy and apathy,
Stare on in disbelief
And streams of tears cascade
Over waterfalls of grief.

Pandora's Box falls open and we step back in awe
And wonder what in Heaven's name
Is all this fighting for?
And building in his wilderness great monuments to sin,
The heathen shakes God's golden gates
And pleads to be let in.

Young heroes die together, old villains live apart,
We speak of love thy neighbour
But hate still fills our hearts,
Forgotten or forgiven, dark tyranny endures,
Long memory and swift vengeance,
Are they mine, or are they yours?

It's only one small step, just another grain of sand
From Once upon a Time, to Never-Never Land.
All those castles in the air, all the fallout from the blast,
All the secrets that we keep, all the stones that we may cast,
Still mean nothing in the end, have no reason and no rhyme,
Falling out of Never-Never Land to Once upon a Time,
Falling out of Never-Never Land to Once upon a Time.

Elegy

An evil smiling archer aims red arrowheads on fire,
Burning black to cinders all the saints upon his pyre,
Now reaching out to grasp safe hands still stretching taut the wire,
Balancing small quaint new-painted faces of the choir.

For now dark orange clouds are swirling high above our heads,
They need to find a resting place among the living dead,
Between the far-flung provinces where broken prophets kneel,
To curse our Earth that scorned their birth and stopped their spinning wheel.

Through sad mystic harmonies, long melancholy songs,
Mad, magic, tragic symphonies dividing right from wrong
Are played through frayed and tattered winds on sailing ships of old,
That roll and pitch love's perfect witch who sold our world for gold.

If heaven's just a sacred milestone on this lonely road,
Each step you take through iron gates where legionnaires once rode,
Is fixed betwixt once gallant ships whose rotting hulks now must,
Try roll and pitch hate's cursed witch who turned our world to dust.

Four mighty horses that once pulled glad Time Lords going home
In heavy jewelled chariots through avenues of stone,
Were stranded and abandoned by time's fickle whim of fate,
To throw the switch no wicked witch can cast her last spell late.

Ghost of a Ploughman
Or Fair Poppy Fields of France

When jingoism swayed me to patriotic fervour
And posters so ubiquitous drove enthusiasm further,
Kitchener's pointing finger declared the Empire surely needs me,
I signed up quick, and agreed to go where King and Country lead me;
To be on the side of victory and justice for my God,
Not an unknown soldier in a lonely cemetery, a piece of cannon fodder.

Then the noises of battle flooded my ears
Like an avalanche in my head
And surrounded me with blood-curdling screams,
From the dying and the dead,
And the air was so foul, like breathing soup,
Bursting my lungs like the devil's embrace,
While the ripping hail sought to impale me,
Like shards of glass on my face.

Then every trench had the stench of death,
From battered, bitter corpses,
While every man fought for every breath,
Among dismembered, bloated horses,
I was tramping in my trench-foot boots,
In the mud and the blood, and skinny starving rats,
There was only one exit from this hell
And it's not shown on the general's maps.

When the last whistle blew we flew over the top,
Brothers in arms, and yet we all know
Kitchener's a lying, warmongering bastard,
Now why did we say we would go?
Oh Yes! We were persuaded to join up
When they led all our boys a merry old dance,
And all we are now are the ghosts of a ploughman
In the fair poppy fields of France.

Love

"We fell, we flew, we always knew."

1. Song to Annis	Written February 1973
2. A Kiss Goodnight	Written 19th April, 2012
3. Honywood Oak	Written 12th August, 2007
4. Tuesday Universe	Written June, 2004
5. Departures	Written 19th/22nd February 2012
6. Wooden Bridge	Written 18th May, 2004

There are probably more poems and songs written on the theme of love than anything else. So here are a few of my contributions, covering a time frame of nearly 40 years. "Song to Annis" was the first love song I wrote which I thought was worth keeping. "A Kiss Goodnight" is an attempt at a villanelle. Most of my poetry rhymes, so "Honywood Oak" is a non-rhyming experiment. The remaining three items adequately fill the "wistful" category.

Song to Annis.

Sixteen summers passed,
And you came along at last,
Someone that I'd been waiting for so long,
And you put your hand in mine;
We drank that good life wine
Just for a while, together we belonged.

Annis every morning I rise with your name upon my lips
And I'll be thinking of you all day long.
Annis there's a bird that flies
the reddest of our sunset skies,
Winging homeward,
Bringing you this song.

Daisy chains were spun
In the Summer sun;
Though the seeds were sown in crisp, white winter days,
The balance was so fine,
Our chance to fill the time,
With flowers gathered from our narrow ways.

Annis every morning I rise with your name upon my lips
And I'll be thinking of you all day long.
Annis there's a bird that flies
the reddest of our sunset skies,
Winging homeward,
Bringing you this song.

You surely were aware,
The time drew ever nearer
For only lonely days when you'd be gone.
You were so very young,
Your journey had just begun
And one day soon you'd want to travel on.

Annis every morning I rise with your name upon my lips
And I'll be thinking of you all day long,
Annis there's a bird that flies
the reddest of our sunset skies,
Winging homeward,
Bringing you this song.

A Kiss Goodnight

A kiss goodnight is all I ask
to soothe me to my sleep,
If that is not too hard a task.

A tipple from your loving flask
to savour and to keep,
A kiss goodnight is all I ask.

And then within your smile I bask
as through the night I creep,
If that is not too hard a task.

Before I slip behind night's mask
and pretend to be Bo-peep,
A kiss goodnight is all I ask.

And hoping that the moment lasts,
I go off counting sheep,
If that is not too hard a task.

When my slumbers have come to pass
and I awake from the deep,
A kiss goodnight was all I asked,
If that was not too hard a task.

Honywood Oak

As two children in a nearly empty but welcoming playground,
We explore and make adventure among the whispering boughs
and rustling leaves,
Soft damp grass beneath our feet, perfect mirror skies above our heads
and fairy nymphs flitting through the sunbeams,
Watching as we smile and enjoy being together.

We stroll beside the placid looking-glass lake and gently lapping waterfalls,
Uncovering the aromatic secrets in the seclusion of a high-walled garden,
Absorbing the luscious coolness of the fern-frond shade
And listening across the meadow green
to the excited chatter of a wedding party.

As we marvel at the history hiding canopy of a tree as old as time,
A silent watching witness to the passage of the years,
Gathering seasons and yearning for the freedom of the skies above,
Through Winter snows, in Spring buds, in Summer, proud and abundant,
And in Autumn changing as the myriad of colours falls and dies.

To touch this miracle, we two children of the Universe
are at one with the tree's perseverance and our transience;
But we have here tried to understand how it feels to be so close to God.

Tuesday Universe

Like a brooding Summer storm,
My thoughts turn to you, in ev'rythin' I do;
Your footsteps dancin' soft across my heart.
I want to kiss your eyes in the mornin' light,
Stay with you babe in the night,
In a Tuesday Universe where the air lies still.

When I open my eyes I see your face,
I want to hold you when you're fast asleep
And watch you body rise and gently fall.
I've fallen in love with you so deep,
You're there in ev'ry breath I breathe,
In a Tuesday Universe where love stands tall.

We fell, we flew, we always knew
we'd soar the skies in perfect blue,
Set stars as precious stones to light the way.
If each hour could have ten thousand days
And each day could have ten thousand hours,
I'd forsake them all to be with you today.

Departures

Platform 4 on the edge of the morning,
Slamming doors, whistle-blown warning,
Thunder roars, ground shakes, wheels squealing,
Fare thee well my love, so sad to know you're leaving.

Was it just wishful thinking?
You blew me a kiss
as the train whistled by in the steam and the smoke
and the crisp morning air shrouded in mists
of the memories we shared.
Were you there,
Or just somewhere else, deep down in my imagination?
I miss you, I miss you, I miss you.

Did I see your thin smile flash by in the window?
Tears rolling down my cheeks in a torrent of sorrow,
A trick of the light in the hot smoky shadows,
Destination tomorrow, loud locomotive echoes.

Was it just wishful thinking?
You blew me a kiss
as the train whistled by in the steam and the smoke
and the crisp morning air shrouded in mists
of the memories we shared.
Were you there,
Or just somewhere else, deep down in my imagination?
I miss you, I miss you, I miss you.

Did you take a last quick glance, for the hint of a slim chance,
A soft whispered whimsy, a flicker of nuance?
Were you stealing a glimpse, a swift flight of fancy,
Lamenting our last dance, eclipse of a romance?

Yes! It was just wishful thinking,
You blew me a kiss
as the train whistled by in the steam and the smoke
and the crisp morning air shrouded in mists
of the memories we shared.
You weren't there,
But just hidden somewhere, deep in my imagination,
I miss you, I miss you, I miss you.

Wooden Bridge

We stood upon a wooden bridge,
In voices soft and hushed,
Cool and opaque a mirror lake
wherein white water rushed,
Tall trees leaned in a circle
and watched our tender touch,
Forever waited at the sides,
And in between, just us.

A bird sang in the willow,
Ducks paddled muddy edge;
Below a tumbling stream flowed on,
Falling from ledge to ledge
And all the while you held me tight,
Time balanced on a ridge,
Forever waited at the sides,
As we stood on the bridge.

We peeped into God's Eden,
A garden perfect made,
Two children of the Universe,
Cascading through the shade.
My heartbeat set a rhythm;
I heard you softly sigh,
Forever held a long sweet breath,
And waited at our sides.

Upon the wings of nowhere,
Two heavens merged as one,
Just us, suspended somewhere,
Two dewdrops in the sun;
A summer breeze warm whispered,
Tall reeds began to sway,
Forever's patience tried too long
And the moment slipped away.

Chuckle and Smile

"If only I'd been more careful with that."

What's funny? Everybody's sense of humour is different, and in this age of political correctness we are all involuntarily restricted in what we can say (and think?). There are no gut-busting laughs here, but just a few observational pieces that might tickle your fancy. There are a few stories written from personal experience on a range of subjects, a touch of nonsense, and some other bits and pieces for your pleasure.

Saturday night flight.

When I saw you at the disco last Saturday night,
Dressed just like a virgin in your perfect white,
And I saw right through your t-shirt in the ultraviolet light,
I felt as if I could, and you looked as if you might.

I thought you were the girl for me,
But I was too blind to see.
I really thought you were the girl for me.

I had a few more lagers till I felt a bit pissed,
Then I said to myself, “It's time to take the risk.”
So I boogied up towards you in a beery hazy mist
And said, “What's a nice girl like you doing in a place like this?”

I thought you were the girl for me,
But I was too pissed to see.
I really thought you were the girl for me.

This pathetic little chat-up line you didn't seem to mind,
So we danced a while together closely entwined,
But I really didn't know that you had something more in mind,
To get me horizontal for some bump and grind.

I thought you were the girl for me,
But I was too blind to see.
I really thought you were the girl for me.

We sped off in my dad's Cortina at the speed of light
And parked in some secluded spot at dead of night,
You said to me, “Let's get in the back.” and I said, “Alright”,
When you had your wicked way with me I nearly died of fright.

I thought you were the girl for me,
But I was too blind to see.
I really thought you were the girl for me.

I found out pretty quickly that I wasn't in your class,
But there I was about to get my end away at last,
“What precautions have you taken?” suddenly you asked,
I said, “It's all right 'cause I have strapped a plank across my arse.”

I thought you were the girl for me,
But I was too blind to see.
I really thought you were the girl for me.

I tried to drive you home, but I was pissed up to the eyes,
We'd only gone a mile or two when I was breathalysed,
I said, “Oh that’s fucking charming.” You said, “Don’t be so surprised.”
One way or the other you must pay for the ride.

I thought you were the girl for me,
But I was too blind to see.
I really thought you were the girl for me.

So bang went my virginity, my poor old heart just sank,
And if you pulled that trick again I'd have to say, “No thanks!”
And if that's what all the fuss is about, I'd rather have a cup of tea,
Unless of course you happen to have six million in the bank.

'Cause then you'd be the girl for me,
And that's a stone cold certainty,
I'd really know you were the girl for me.

Margery's old car

Some people get turned on by cars, all shiny, fast and new,
On TV, Jeremy Clarkson drives more than a few,
But there is a special motor car more likely to appear,
Upon the Antiques Roadshow, rather than Top Gear,
So if I've got you baffled with what this song's about,
I'll give to you just one more clue, for you to work it out,
It's sitting in the car park, and you know that ain't so far,
I refer of course to the old workhorse that is Margery's old car.

Intrepid travellers they are, and record breakers too,
Michael Palin and Richard Branson wondered what to do,
They pondered on a joint attempt at some new startling deed,
Palin to go far and wide, and Branson to succeed,
For many days they sat around devoid of inspiration,
No ideas could they dream up to fire the imagination,
And all at once up in the sky, there came a shooting star,
"I know we'll go round the world in Margery's old car."

All the escapologists were at a World Convention,
Swapping tricks, and politics, and hiding their intentions,
In David Copperfield's best trick, six elephants disappeared,
The illusion had us all enthralled, loud and long we cheered,
Houdini was in great distress, his reputation gone,
He just had to be the best, and never be outdone,
But his new trick was up his sleeve and confirmed him as a star,
When all six elephants re-appeared in Margery's old car.

There was a poor old gentleman, alone and feeling sad,
Week after week, he tried to eke, the pension out he had,
And then he won the Lottery, more than he'd ever dared,
He'd live a life of luxury; no expense would be spared,
They asked him what he would prefer, a Porsche or Lamborghini,
You've got the dosh, so go all posh, no need to be a meanie,
He said, "I am not interested; I've been OK so far.
I've made an offer that can't be refused for Margery's old car."

Julio Iglesias was on the Morning Show,
About his long career in song, they didn't want to know,
To Richard and to Judy too, it couldn't be ignored,
He was supposed to have made love to a thousand women or more.
They questioned and cajoled him, 'til he became quite vexed,
"After all that song and sex, Well! Whatever next?"
He said," I've one ambition left for swinging on a star,
"To make love to my new girlfriend in Margery's old car."

On Saturday Margery was meeting with her mates,
The rain came down in buckets, boredom arrived in crates,
Her friends were sad and so depressed, with no relief in sight,
But she refused to be impressed, without some kind of fight,
Margery was positive; she'd turn the gloom about,
If life was tough, she knew enough, to quickly sort it out,
"I've got the cure; I know for sure, you'll cheer up when we are,
All going to the Southend seaside in Margery's old car."

Talkin' bollocks

Touchin' forelocks,
Greetin' the man with no name,
Talkin' bollocks,
Talkin' bollocks once again.

Wreakin' havoc,
Stirrin' it up with no shame,
Talkin' bollocks,
Talkin' bollocks once again.

Smokin' haddocks,
Sizzlin' over blue flames,
Talkin' bollocks,
Talkin' bollocks once again.

Bulging stomachs,
Feastin' till you're in pain,
Talkin' bollocks,
Talkin' bollocks once again.

Talkin' bollocks,
Usin' my Indian name,
Yeah, talkin' bollocks,
Talkin' bollocks once again.

Colchester Hospital

Radiotherapy, appointments to keep,
Fifteen visits to make, every day for three weeks,
A fifty mile round-trip from Chelmsford by car,
To irradiate you, to make sure you are
Freed from the curs'd cells that dumped you in this hell.

Colchester Hospital, car park too small,
You queue in the rain, by the bin that is full
With fag-ends discarded
By the people who won't give up their bad habit
For the people who don't want to breathe in the stain
That's polluting their brain.

Car park attendant stands there and grins
Inanely, insanely, 'til he guides you in
To a space he selects on the visitor's row,
As ambulance cars they come and they go,
While you wait there confused
By the man's entry booth.

Colchester Hospital; it feels so wrong,
As you drive there and back,
Taking four times as long as the fifteen minutes treatment,
Fifteen minutes of burn.
If only it was fifteen minutes before you return!
For fifteen minutes lying in that radiated space;
Sometimes it takes twice as long
To find a parking space.

An Autumn invitation to Halloween Danger Cake (You need to be careful with that)

On the 31st of October
There's an annual young gangster regime
Of fake zombies rising from their graves
To celebrate Halloween.
It maybe only one night in the year
When demons stalk your street,
Dressed up as ghouls or skeletons,
Ready for trick or treat,
But underneath the Asda costume,
Hidden in the folklore bluff and mist,
Is a miniature part time criminal - a trainee terrorist.
That gentle, stage-managed persuasion
To bribe them with chocolate or sweets;
Well, you know you need to be careful with that
When they're playing trick or treat.
And it wouldn't do to be saying,
"I wish I'd been quicker on my feet,
If only I'd been more careful with that."
When they were playing trick or treat.

When Summer has crashed down to its knees
And hides behind a rising wall,
The swirling winds and turning leaves
Bid hello and welcome to the Fall -
Red, gold, and yellow tumbling leaves
Show Autumn's colourful splash;
A letter box rattles in the wind,
As a wily fox raids dustbin trash.
Warm overcoats are dusted off
With scarves and hats and gloves,
As icy rain comes lashing down
From the angry grey skies above,
Quick season's clock goes ticking by
To measure out it's changing ways,
Well, you know you need to be careful with that,
And treasure every one of your passing days.
And it wouldn't do to be saying,
“I wish I'd been more wise in my ways,
If only I'd been more careful with that,
And treasured every one of my days.”

When we had barbecues in the gardens
And enjoyed black, char-grilled food;
Had picnics in the primrose wood,
Went swimming in the nude,
Had birthday party bouncy castles,
And wedding reception celebrations,
Funeral wakes with fancy cakes,
And graduation invitations,
There were Valentine's Day flowers
And Easter Eggs and bunnies were found,
Boxes of chocs, and novelty socks,
When Christmastime came around;
But I'm not sure about this strange invite,
If this kind of bash is really for me?
Well, you know you need to be careful with that,
I've never been to that kind of party.
And it wouldn't do to be saying,
"I wish I'd been not quite so flash,
If only I'd been more careful with that,
Invite to a swinger's bash."

She stood in the kitchen completely alone,
Comfortably dressed in a onesy.
She had a request to do her best,
To bake some currant bunsy.
That definitely wasn't her forte;
She had better things to make,
It was nicer to be naughty
And to arrange for a danger cake.
All the ingredients were assembled
And she started to mix and to bake
And added that extra secret touch,
That's essential for danger cake.
You're going to be taking your life in your hands,
You may vanish without a trace;
Well, you know you need to be careful with that,
In case it explodes in your face.
And it wouldn't do to be saying,
"Why I only had one slice,
If only I'd been more careful with that -
But danger cake's far too nice."

Courgette (The story of Cheryl and Pete)

She was a cheeky, curvaceous and charming courgette,
Looking for love on the Internet;
Gorgeous and green and obviously willing
Were her admirable credentials
And a good sense of humour in her beau,
Were her vegetable essentials.

But the trawl through the trash on the websites for dating,
Just made her despair for that longed-for perfect mating.
She was plagued with no-hopers, in all shapes and sizes,
A motley crew,
But what can you do with vegetables that don't win prizes?

Cauliflowers from Carlisle, and sweet potatoes from Peru,
Curly kale from Skelmersdale, and tomatoes and shoots of bamboo,
Bok Choy and choi sum, mustard greens and parsnips,
Artichokes from Jerusalem and soya beans and turnips,
Lettuces from Latvia and kohlrabi from Tehran,
A mange tout from Montpelier, an aubergine from the Sudan.

There was broccoli and endives and radishes and beets,
Brussels sprouts and asparagus and a few shallots and leeks,
Mustard greens from the Philippines, carrots, celery and okra,
Onions, spinach, parsnips, garlic, mung beans and alfalfa,
Cucumbers from Chicago,
Peppers and avocados,
Chard, mooli and collard greens,
Watercress and green beans.

A sadness descended upon her,
She began to weep and to howl,
Her search had gone on far too long,
She was just about to throw in the trowel.

And then she found the perfect match, a pumpkin boy from Plaistow,
Her joy was overwhelming when she found her love at last, oh!

They were married in Malibu in a mad whirlwind romance,
And honeymooned in Heaven in a lovely chateau in France,
They set up home in Norfolk, in a semi in Kings Lynn,
And later that year they were proud to be,
The parents of Zucchini twins.

Philosophical?

"The horizon is always just out of reach."

1. All you can become	Written 20th August, 2002
2. Moments	Written Magaluf, Majorca 7th February 2000
3. Lost	Written 22nd February, 1998
4. Horizon (for Rosalind)	Written 12th September 1999
5. Waiting room	Written 29th January 2000
6. Good Intentions	Written 10th July 1999

Maybe it's a bit of a hobby, but when I read back things I've written, I often find a bit of potted philosophy (or is it potty?). Here's a little sampling from the thoughts of Chairman Mick, concluding with a piece called "Good Intentions (A Letter to the Planet)" which sums up just about everything.

All you can become

And in the end my friend,
All you can become
Is the sum of all the words you've said
And all the deeds you've done;
Of everyone you've ever met
And everything you've seen;
The depths of your experience
And the places you have been.

Your value is in who you are;
How you became that way
And one day you may understand
Why it has to be that way.

Of every blade that cut you
And every word that soothed;
Of all the times your heart stood still
And the times your spirit moved.

Your value is in who you are;
How you became that way
And one day you may understand
Why it has to be that way.

Of all the love that you poured out
And gathered in together;
Of every breath you ever breathed
And every trial endeavoured.

Your value is in who you are,
How you became that way
And one day you may understand
Why it has to be that way.

And in the end you know my friend,
What you'll become is not
The sum of all your treasures
And the riches you have got.

Your value is in who you are,
How you became that way
And when you understand my friend
I've nothing more to say.

Moments

The distant laughter of children at play in life without a care,
The contented purr of a marmalade cat lazing on your chair,
The cool whisper of desert sands caressed by a moonlight kiss,
The fleeting smile of a blushing bride in her new-wedded bliss,
The silent flight of an Autumn leaf fluttering down from above,
The instant joy you feel the first time you're in love,
Moments, perfect moments, stolen and soon lost,
Moments, magic moments, fading into dust,
Moments, precious moments, here, then quickly gone,
Moments, priceless moments, never held for long,
Moments, we're just moments, only here to be,
Moments, just a heartbeat, from eternity.

The electric spark that lights the senses as a new idea arrives,
The patient pulse of the cooling breath keeping you alive,
The silver sun shimmering and dancing on a softly lapping sea,
The secret kiss of a fragrant breeze among the tall green trees,
The sweet morning dew on the lushest grass soothing tiny toes,
The knowing look of a special friend that says our love still grows,
Moments, perfect moments, stolen and soon lost,
Moments, magic moments, fading into dust,
Moments, precious moments, here, then quickly gone,
Moments, priceless moments, never held for long,
Moments, we're just moments, only here to be,
Moments, just a heartbeat from eternity.

The crystals of rain on a window pane that run and disappear,
The gossamer twirl of a fairy cloud floating high and clear,
The quiet knock of a tick-tocking clock measuring out the day,
The last few rays of a dying sun throwing crimson across the bay,
The flicker flame of a warm log fire glowing in a winter hearth,
The sad long sigh that skips a beat in a lover's broken heart,
Moments, perfect moments, stolen and soon lost,
Moments, magic moments, fading into dust,
Moments, precious moments, here, then quickly gone,
Moments, priceless moments, never held for long,
Moments, we're just moments, only here to be,
Moments, just a heartbeat, from eternity.

Lost

Yesterday's a distant valley where I spent some time,
Today's a rugged mountain that I still have to climb;
Tomorrow is a winding trail that chance or choice embraces
And time is a mysterious river running through these places.

Narrow trails have brought our quest to a crossroads with no sign,
The road ahead is damned or blessed so many hills to climb;
Where is the bridge that we must cross to stand on solid ground?
For in this moment we are lost by the instant we have found.

Whilst rust encrusted hinges swing trapdoors to and fro
Between the places we have been and those we've yet to go,
Thin doors of opportunity for moments remain open,
Snap shut so quick behind us the instant they are taken.

There's but one path to chart this course, though there are many stations
And all is clear we steer towards one constant destination,
For many are the trials of life and many are its glories,
And chances to glance back in time for each to tell their stories.

Along the way delayed by pain, grief, consternation and stress
Sometimes we suffer at the hands of things that bring distress.
From opposites, on tortuous routes our common journeys spin;
In truth we know there's one way out, as there was one way in.

Why try to bind us both with love's elusive secret treasure?
We are not then, we're only now, but we will be forever,
For love is all that can stand tall, for love provides the measure,
When we are just then, no longer now, we will still be forever.

Horizon (for Rosalind)

The horizon is not at the end of your nose,
Or the tips of your fingers, or tips of your toes;
The horizon is set at the end of a rainbow.

In placid blue waters moving quiet and lazy,
In rugged red deserts shimmering rude and remote,
In lush, warm, green forests spreading far past your gaze,
In sleek silver clouds floating high and aloof,
In distant white mountains guarding treasures undreamed of,
In precious gold sunsets blazing day's glorious end.

The horizon's as far as your mind's eye perceives,
It's as wide as the truths in which you believe,
It's as high as the ideals you seek to achieve,
It's as deep as the sorrow you feel when you grieve,
It's as big as the love that you give and receive.

The horizon is always just out of reach;
It's as bitter as vinegar, sweet as a peach -
An elusive illusion beyond pure extremes,
To bring into focus our hopes and our dreams.

Waiting room

Oh, how did I come here?
Did I surrender too soon?
Sitting in silence
In the waiting room;
Paying my penance,
In the waiting room;
Searching my conscience
In the waiting room;
Fearing for vengeance,
In the waiting room;
Praying for deliverance,
In the waiting room.

Dim light casting shadows,
Dark shapes in the gloom,
No doors and no windows,
In the waiting room;
Suspended in limbo,
In the waiting room;
A sad desperado,
In the waiting room;
Narrow and shallow,
In the waiting room;
Down to ground zero,
In the waiting room.

Oh, where will I go now;
To salvation or doom?
To what destination,
From the waiting room?
Can I escape back to living
Knowing I will return?
Do I fall through the floor
Forever to burn?
Do I stay here forever
For eternity?
Will I be blown to the four winds;
Scattered debris?
Or perhaps there's no need,
To fear damnation or doom;
I will fly free into the sky,
From the waiting room.

Good Intentions

Jimi smiled through Voodoo Child and Janis sang the blues,
Poseidon rose up from the deep and brought fantastic news,
He read out from an autocue, as ageing soap stars wept,
To mourn the few unfortunates whose secrets were not kept
Away from prying ears and eyes whose horoscopes foretell
Of incidents and accidents along the road to Hell.

Down at the local gay bar the waltzing lovers mince
In leather jackets and feather hats they've stolen from a prince,
Who used to rule the kingdom of the blind misunderstood
From a sacred throne of shattered bones secluded in a wood;
The champagne breakfast Concorde flight crash lands on my hotel,
Before I change direction and then take the road to Hell.

In the hall of mirrors Pinocchio is choosing a new nose
From catalogues of plastic surgery and sexual bondage clothes;
But there are only silent films on afternoon TV,
To wake the dead where angels tread to solve the mystery
Why Roald Dahl and Stephen King crack open oyster shells,
To sell to travelling salesmen driving on the road to Hell.

The stamp collecting paedophiles sign on the Internet,
Looking for child ballerinas and first day cover sets;
Wild rhythms of loud jungle drums swing Tarzan through the air,
To rescue Jane from certain death in the electric chair;
The eye in the sky forever spies as road-rage bandits yell
That no one knows where ill winds blow along the road to Hell.

Down at the derelict hospital the registrar's asleep;
Most patients down in A & E have waited for a week;
And only when the fire alarm is smashed in desperation,
Then doctors sneak back from the bar next to the railway station.
The silence of the lambs is shattered by the tolling bells,
And all the houses have no doors along the road to Hell.

Oscar Wilde lays in the gutter outside of Reading Gaol,
As three wise monkeys tempted him to pull the donkey's tail,
But he was looking at the stars with his telescope extended,
As ladies of the night paraded and Siamese twins pretended
That the tooth fairy could be busted out from her padded cell.
So she could make her breakaway along the road to Hell.

Tough cowboys on their campfire trail cook up their pork 'n beans
And voodoo jazzmen improvise down in New Orleans;
And when the sun's eclipsed again by choking black smokestacks,
Express delivery pizza boys arrive with tasty snacks,
While chocolate Easter Bunny witches cast their evil spells
And no one cares who shines the lamps that light the road to Hell.

The long arm of the law reached out and drew the shortest straw,
As juvenile delinquents plotted red in tooth and claw
To overthrow the dynasty that rules with iron fists
The people's lands and ragged bands of guerrillas in their midst,
Just as double glazing salesmen call with windows for their cells
And all the unmarked cars arrive that drive the road to Hell.

Fat geriatric rock-chicks wake on a tequila sunrise day,
And in the green room lesbian thespians are rehearsing for a play;
The Hotel California's full with Arthur's gallant knights,
Spielberg hands out bars of gold to secure the movie rights,
But no man is the wiser for what causes that bad smell,
That chokes my throat and stings my eyes along the road to Hell.

Frankenstein drinks vintage wine with the woman in the moon,
Neil Armstrong takes a giant leap across the blue lagoon,
Tutankhamen throws a curse and grave robbers are running scared
Across the sun-baked desert sands for times still undeclared
When the Orient Express arrives from lands where devils dwell,
You know that there are tolls to pay along the road to Hell.

So when the mushroom farmers meet to auction their new crop,
Black horses in green valleys laugh until the bidding stops,
And soon the judge and jury sit to contemplate your crimes,
Then it's too late to change your fate and travel back in time,
'Cause you and I will know the time has come to pay our bill,
But they don't take cheques and credit cards along the road to Hell.

Miscellaneous

"My ransom's paid for summer days."

1. Molly Brown's Blues — Written May, 1998

2. Saloon Girl's Kiss — Written 3rd February 2001

3. Wicked Angels, Luscious Demons — Written 1st/3rd December 2011

4. Dangerous Curves — Written 5th/10th April 2012

5. Something Else
(A load of rambling nonsense about something other than the colours of the rainbow) — Written 3rd/6th May 2013

This section covers a multitude of evils, or is it that they don't fit easily into a clearly defined category? Molly Brown was a hero of the Titanic disaster, Saloon Girl's Kiss is a tale of the Wild West, and Wicked Angels is a bit of a fantasy piece. Dangerous Curves was the catalyst for the writing of my two novels based in Chelmsford in the year 2012. Something Else is as it says; a load of rambling nonsense about something other than the colours of the rainbow.

So that's it!

Molly Brown's Blues

One day we set sail
On the maiden voyage of the Titanic,
Disaster is unthinkable,
The ship is unsinkable,
Icebergs are harmless,
Lifeboats superfluous;
We will survive,
Nevertheless, I'd hazard a guess.

That day we set sail
On the maiden voyage of the Titanic,
The vessel is invincible,
To think the unthinkable,
Icebergs are due,
Lifeboats too few;
We might survive,
Nevertheless, I'd hazard a guess.

If again we set sail
On the maiden voyage of the Titanic,
It's fearful to think,
This vessel can sink,
Icebergs inevitable,
Lifeboats un-gettable;
Survival not certain,
Nevertheless, I'd hazard a guess.

Yet again we set sail
On the maiden voyage of the Titanic,
This time we assume,
This vessel is doomed,
Icebergs in waves,
No lifeboats to save us;
Survival in doubt,
Nevertheless, I'd hazard a guess.

There will be as many rides
On the maiden voyage of the Titanic,
As you need to convince you,
No ship is unsinkable,
Always another iceberg,
Never enough lifeboats,
You cannot survive;
Nevertheless, the answer I guess.
The only thing unsinkable,
On the maiden voyage of the Titanic -

Was Molly Brown.

Saloon Girl's Kiss

Luke was a cool and handsome dude,
A gunslingin' gamblin' man,
With his fancy suits and snakeskin boots,
He rode out of Cheyenne,
He rode out of Cheyenne.

Miss Kitty was a whore in Wichita,
So well she played her game.
They never knew her real name was Jude,
The dudes who paid and came,
The dudes who paid and came.

When a gamblin' man's days are over and done,
Well, he lives for the whiskey
And dies by the gun,
While the cards keep a-rollin'
And the bullets still miss;
There ain't nothin' so sweet as a saloon girl's kiss.

Luke was slick with that bottom card trick,
Aces high and smokin' guns,
Fast guns and sharp cards from across the Wild West,
Tried to end his winnin' run,
Tried to end his winnin' run.

Every day at sundown, the boys rode into town
To get their whiskey kicks,
Them cowboys came from many a mile,
To buy one of Miss Kitty's tricks,
To buy one of Miss Kitty's tricks.

When a gamblin' man's days are over and done,
Well, he lives for the whiskey
And dies by the gun,
While the cards keep a-rollin'
And the bullets still miss;
There ain't nothin' so sweet as a saloon girl's kiss.

Down at the Crazy Horse Saloon,
When gamblin' men came to play,
That's where Luke the dude met a gal called Jude,
She never made him pay,
She never made him pay.

Bordello born, Luke's baby girl,
As the midnight moon came round,
And in an ambush trick Luke bit the dust,
They shot that cool dude down,
They shot that cool dude down.

When a gamblin' man's days are over and done,
Well, he lives for the whiskey
And dies by the gun,
While the cards keep a-rollin'
And the bullets still miss;
There ain't nothin' so sweet as a saloon girl's kiss.

She grew up poor, but she grew up proud,
Her mamma died when she was thirteen;
She knew for sure where she was headed for,
The same place her mamma had been;
Same place where mamma had been.

Now when times got tough, she just made enough
With cards, and bars, and booze,
And folks rode in from miles around
To hear Nancy sing the blues,
To hear Nancy sing the blues.

Wicked Angels, Luscious Demons

Dark whispers keep my mind at bay,
The jungle hills drum far away,
But in sweet rustle autumn golds
Under wide lonely skies unfold.
Oh peace to keep my mind at rest
And fill the place I love the best;
The glorious sun, brilliant, undimmed,
A balmy breeze, not biting wind;
For chasing angels through the haze,
My ransom's paid for summer days;
Wicked Angels, luscious Demons,
Flying round in my dreams.

The silent slip of twilight's hand
Goes sliding smooth across this land
And rides disguised, into the dawn,
To break the night spell so forlorn.
Oh peace to keep my heart full-blessed
And steal the time I love the best.
The moon's cool shadows wait unspent,
To wonder why and where we went
Just chasing angels through the crowds
And painting rainbows on the clouds;
Wicked Angels, luscious Demons,
Flying round in my dreams.

Whilst mail trains thunder through the night
To cities blazed in neon light,
We sleep entwined and face to face,
Together locked in soft embrace,
At peace to keep our hearts on song,
On Heaven's edge where we belong;
And lost in dreams the Sandman brings
On gentle glides of angel's wings,
We chase our whispers through till morn,
When night's dark curtain shroud is gone;
Wicked Angels, luscious Demons,
Flying round in my dreams.

Dangerous Curves

I'm driving in my Porsche in the dead of night,
Roaring through the countryside, blazing headlights,
Pedal to the metal, squealing tyres and burning rubber,
Shifting through my gears beyond a hundred miles an hour.
I'm your tailgater and I'm bringing up your rear,
I don't want no motorways, no straight roads, or low gears,
Want to feel the G-force, the horsepower, and the swerve;
Man, I'm just a petrol-head on dangerous curves,
Dangerous curves, dangerous curves,
Man, I'm just a petrol-head on dangerous curves,
Running my wheels over dangerous curves,
Showing my skills on dangerous curves,
Moving in for the kill on dangerous curves.
Man, I'm just a petrol-head on dangerous curves.

Dressed up in my finery for nightlife on the pull,
Wallet stuffed with ready cash, attitude full of bull (shit),
Not looking for that special someone - no just a one night stand,
No long term commitment babes, no-one ties my hands.
I'm God's gift to women; you know I'm the man,
Got the looks, got the dosh, ain't no also-ran;
No computer dating, can't get what I deserve,
Looking for a lady with dangerous curves,
Dangerous curves, dangerous curves,
Looking for a lady with dangerous curves,
Kissing and caressing those dangerous curves,
Counting my blessings for dangerous curves,
Ain't doing no confessing on dangerous curves.
Looking for a lady with dangerous curves.

I went to see the doctor; I was feeling below par,
Drove there at breakneck speed in my turbo-charged car,
He fixed monitor wires to my body and my head,
He umm'd and ah'd, and took some notes and this is what he said,
"I've been looking at your test results, so let's not pretend,
Someone here's been burning the candle at both ends;
You'd better slow down my friend; you've been living on your nerves,
There's overwhelming evidence for dangerous curves.
Dangerous curves, dangerous curves,
There's overwhelming evidence for dangerous curves,
Live fast, die young, on dangerous curves,
Won't last too long on dangerous curves,
One day you'll die on dangerous curves.
There's overwhelming evidence for dangerous curves.

Something Else (A load of rambling nonsense about something other than the colours of the rainbow).

I was asked to write a piece to be called, “Something Else.”
But every time I tried my thoughts were cast aside
By an another idea that was languishing on the shelf,
That wouldn't go away, and held me in its sway,
In the grip of a dilemma for day after day.

When I picked up the pen the words would not flow,
And the keyboard just collected the dust,
Words tangled my fingers, the agony lingers,
To resolve this problem I must
Begin to write what I know, about the colours of the rainbow.

The first idea that I could find in the dark recesses of my mind,
Was not the ROYGBIV that my memory jars,
So they say Richard Of York Gave Battle In Vain,
But what I thought about was green cars;
And how they've taken over from the reds and the blacks,
And possibly the silvers in the future;
They come in many shades, fashioned and made,
In any tint or hint of green that'll suit yer.

So beware of people who drive green cars,
If you'd care to see they strive too far
To prove their essentials are green and true,
By moving their credentials into my view,
But they still use petrol and diesel too,
Why not? It's good enough for me and you.

Can it really be that to drive a green car means it's ecologically sound?
If the driver can't see over the steering wheel, as the other four wheels go round and round,
And if it's electric that's totally pathetic, because it actually powered by fossil fuels we're burning,
Yet they wave and they smile for mile upon mile, when the wind turbine has stopped turning.
No, beware of people who drive green cars,
Eco warriors they'll claim to be,
Whilst laying the blame for the global warm
On the likes of you and me.

Now, beware of people who wear brown shoes,
If you'd care to see that it's more bad news;
Leather when tanned is naturally brown
Whether the cow was standing or lying down.

Beware of people who don red hats;
If you care to see what's wrong with that;
A saying that cannot be ignored
Suggests a red hat means they're wearing no drawers.

In a world where white elephants are everywhere
There are pink flamingos and mad March hares,
There are great crested newts and cute little voles,
Blue whales, giant snails and smooth skinned moles,
The great white shark and grey Canada geese,
But no blue giraffes or purple wildebeest.

Now at last to the matter of the colours of the rainbow,
I'll lay them on a platter, in the order that you know.

Beware of people who wear red hats and shoes,
Red sails in the sunset is much better news.
Steer clear of secret eaters of duck a l'orange,
Especially in France where they don't eat, they mange.
Avoid anybody with a yellow bunch of roses,
"I'm leaving you darling." are the words that it proposes.
As I've said, beware of people who drive green motors,
Especially those that are Green Party voters.
Don't go dancing with people in blue suede shoes,
And please don't step on them, whatever you do.
Now indigo is something with which you shouldn't bother,
Except in the rainbow there no such colour.
Of people who eat Parma violets you must remain aware;
They've reached the end of the rainbow and you don't need to go there,
Even if you're looking for a pot of gold,
You won't find one there, even though it's been foretold.

And so my friends before you go,
There's something else that you should know,
While we may talk of worlds and waterfalls,
And gaze amazed at crystal balls
And deliberate at rights and wrongs
And read our books and sing our songs;
In the great realm of things,
In the daily grind,
The Oracle may have changed his mind.
He's concerned that we must surely know
There's something else before we go;
Here are words of wisdom for you to find,
Exploring colours in your mind.

Wise Words?

"It happens to the best of us"

1. Really?	Written circa 2000
2. Maxim	Written circa February, 2002
3. Thoughts on Love	Written 11th/12th November 2006
4. It happens to the best of us	Written circa 1975
5. Goodbye!	Written 19th November, 2003

I leave you with just a few thoughts on a range of subjects. I hope this lot have whetted your appetite for a lot more to come in my forthcoming poetry, songs, stories and other and writings compilation called "Tall Words on a Wall".

Watch this Space!

Really?

The paradox is that there is no paradox,
The best logic is no logic at all.

Maxim

You can't teach an old dog new tricks,
But you can teach old tricks to a new dog.

Thoughts on Love

When offered in truth from the very heart of being, the words "I love you" cannot be weakened or diminished by time, nor adversity, nor the frequency with which they are spoken.

Indeed, whilst the words "I love you" are by themselves supremely powerful, it is love itself that is indisputably strengthened and enlarged by the passage of time, the experiences of adversity, and the frequency of their revelation.

It happens to the best of us

By the time I reach Heaven,
I will probably,
Be dead!
So will you.
Ha! Ha!

Goodbye!

You're born,
You live,
You die,
Goodbye, Goodbye, Goodbye!
You meet,
You love,
You live,
You give,
You try,
You fail,
You fail to try,
Goodbye, Goodbye, Goodbye!

Lightning Source UK Ltd.
Milton Keynes UK
UKOW04f0950040615

252884UK00001B/54/P

9 781910 530641